Abruzzo
Travel Guide

Quick Trips Series

No part of this publication may be reproduced, stored in a retrieval system, or transmitted, in any form or by any means without the prior written permission of the publisher, nor be otherwise circulated in any form of binding or cover other than that in which it is published and without similar condition being imposed on the subsequent purchaser. If there are any errors or omissions in copyright acknowledgements the publisher will be pleased to insert the appropriate acknowledgement in any subsequent printing of this publication. Although we have taken all reasonable care in researching this book we make no warranty about the accuracy or completeness of its content and disclaim all liability arising from its use.

Copyright © 2016, Astute Press
All Rights Reserved.

Table of Contents

ABRUZZO — 5
- 🌐 CUSTOMS & CULTURE 8
- 🌐 GEOGRAPHY 12
- 🌐 WEATHER & BEST TIME TO VISIT 15

SIGHTS & ACTIVITIES: WHAT TO SEE & DO — 17
- 🌐 L'AQUILA 17
- 🌐 TERAMO 19
- 🌐 SULMONA 23
- 🌐 PESCARA 26
- 🌐 CHIETI 28
- 🌐 NATIONAL PARKS 30
- 🌐 CASTLES & FORTRESSES 31
- 🌐 RECOMMENDED ITINERARY: TWO DAYS IN ABRUZZO 33

BUDGET TIPS — 34
- 🌐 ACCOMMODATION 34
  - Hotel Rojan 34
  - Albergo Stella 35
  - Hotel Alba 36
  - Hotel Gran Sasso 37
  - Harri's Hotel Chieti 38
- 🌐 PLACES TO EAT 39

    Carbonera..39
    La Terrazze..40
    La Cucina di Lullo 40
    Riva Reno 41
    Ristorante Pizzeria bar II Sarto Imbocca 42

🌐 SHOPPING 43
    Confetti of Sulmona..43
    Chieti...44
    L'Aquila..44
    Antique Shopping 44
    Centro D'Abruzzo 45

KNOW BEFORE YOU GO   46

🌐 ENTRY REQUIREMENTS 46
🌐 HEALTH INSURANCE..46
🌐 TRAVELLING WITH PETS..47
🌐 AIRPORTS..48
🌐 AIRLINES 49
🌐 CURRENCY..50
🌐 BANKING & ATMS 50
🌐 CREDIT CARDS 50
🌐 TOURIST TAXES 51
🌐 RECLAIMING VAT 52
🌐 TIPPING POLICY 52
🌐 MOBILE PHONES 52
🌐 DIALLING CODE 53
🌐 EMERGENCY NUMBERS 54
🌐 PUBLIC HOLIDAYS 54
🌐 TIME ZONE 55

- 🌐 Daylight Savings Time 55
- 🌐 School Holidays 55
- 🌐 Trading Hours 56
- 🌐 Driving Laws 56
- 🌐 Drinking Laws 57
- 🌐 Smoking Laws 58
- 🌐 Electricity 58
- 🌐 Tourist Information (TI) 58
- 🌐 Food & Drink 59
- 🌐 Websites 60

ABRUZZO TRAVEL GUIDE

Abruzzo

Abruzzo is located 80 kilometres east of Rome in central Italy and extends to the Adriatic Sea. The region is a delight for outdoors lovers and offers sandy beaches, dense forests, national parks and undulating valleys. The hilltop castles, medieval towns and ancient monasteries add to the mystic charm of Abruzzo, which is one of the greenest regions of Europe.

From the mountaintops of the Apennines to the underwater splendor of the Adriatic shores, the range of attractions in Abruzzo is impressive.

In the Middle Ages the region was part of the 'Kingdom of the Two Sicilies' and was divided into 'Nearer Abruzzo'

ABRUZZO TRAVEL GUIDE

and 'Farther Abruzzo I & II' in reference to the distance from the ancient capital of the region, Naples. Abruzzo is now divided into four provinces, L'Aquila, Teramo, Chieti, and Pescara. The capital of the Abruzzo region is the historic city of L'Aquila. Other major cities in the region are Pescara, Chieti, Sulmona, and Teramo.

The country name of Italy's may have originated in Abruzzo where coins from the 1st century BC have been found with the inscription "Italia."

The Abruzzo region attracts millions of tourists every year and tourism is one of the pillars of the local economy. Ecotourism and mountain tourism are both popular given Abruzzo's national parks and other protected areas, more than a dozen ski resorts, good hiking trails, and many other nature-based activities.

ABRUZZO TRAVEL GUIDE

Beach tourism is naturally very popular in this warm part of Europe and Abruzzo has a 129 km coastline on the Adriatic with many beaches carrying the prestigious Blue Flag of safety. Other than sunbathing and swimming, visitors can enjoy fishing, windsurfing, snorkeling, underwater photography and other watersports.

A number of good hotels and resorts on the coast have been developed recently to cater to visitors of various budgets.

Visitors can find interesting religious and art/historical attractions in Abruzzo in the major towns like Pescara as well as in the hilltop villages with their well-preserved castles, monasteries and churches. The Shrine of Gabriel of Our Lady of Sorrows in Teramo attracts more than 2 million visitors every year, making it one of the top 15 sanctuaries in the world.

The region offers something for visitors of all ages. Backpackers will enjoy the raw wilderness, camping and hiking. Others will enjoy the luxuries offered by the numerous spa resorts.

Abruzzo has seen a much economic growth in the last few decades and today it is the richest region in southeastern Italy.

🌐 Customs & Culture

With its rich history and tradition, the Abruzzo region celebrates a number of events and festivals throughout the year.

ABRUZZO TRAVEL GUIDE

The town of Sulmona celebrates Holy Week with much fanfare. Locals carry a statue of Madonna along the streets and the town square towards her resurrected Son. Easter celebrations and rituals take place.

Cocullo, in L'Aquila province has an eccentric festival called the Snake Handler's Procession. Believed to have originated in pre-Roman times, the festival has the statue of St Dominic – the town patron – being carried through the streets while covered with live serpents! This festival is held on the first Thursday in May. The procession ends on a hilltop with a banquet and fireworks. Thousands of pilgrims and tourists gather to watch the festival.

If you are visiting Abruzzo in January, do not miss the Feast of Anthony the Great with its elaborate and scenic bonfires. The Feast is held in many of the towns and villages of the region. Picciano celebrates the Traditional Befana Festival in the same month.

In Rivisondoli, every year the townsfolk re-enact the arrival of the three wise men in the Living Nativity Scene. In Fara Filiorum Petri, the locals celebrate the Farchi Festival where giant torches are illuminated in honor of St Anthony.

In February, Francavilla a Mare celebrates a Carnival Festival while Citta Sant Angelo has a Carnival Parade of Floats.

Good Friday is celebrated through the Frittata Festival in San Valentino. The event is also celebrated with a huge procession in L'Aquila.

ABRUZZO TRAVEL GUIDE

The summer sees numerous festivities. Rocca di Mezzo celebrates the Daffodil Festival on the last Sunday of May. The festival – celebrating the advent of spring – is marked by presentations, folkloric dances, and a parade of flowery floats. During the same month, Bucchianico celebrates the Flower Festival – a re-enactment of a 13th century battle with a parade of miniature floats.

In August, Cappelli Sul Tavo hosts the Palio del Pupo Costume Race. Also in August, Cepagatti hosts an annual historical parade with fireworks, floats, and celebrations.

L'Aquila organizes the Pope Celestino's Pardon Ceremonies. Popoli celebrates the Trout and Shrimp Festival, certainly a celebration with a difference.

ABRUZZO TRAVEL GUIDE

Cappelle Sultano holds a giant puppet parade that culminates with a huge fireworks display. If you are in Scanno in August, you can witness a re-enactment of their distinctive local wedding customs in the Traditional Wedding Ceremony Festival.

Food lovers will enjoy the annual Culinary Festival in Villa Santa Maria. This 3-day festival is held every October and attracts renowned chefs from the region coming together to give demonstrations and workshops.

Abruzzo's cuisine is delicious and there is much to choose from. The local food relies on "peasant dishes" often infused with saffron spice. Lamb and pork dishes are common as is Pecorino (lamb's milk). Try the local goat's milk-cheese or the scamorza cheese. Fish dishes are best on the Adriatic coast of course.

ABRUZZO TRAVEL GUIDE

Italy is known for its lovely wines. In Abruzzo you are spoiled for choice. Start off by trying the red wine, Montepulciano and/or the white wine, Trebbiano.

The importance of food is reflected in various events in Abruzzo. Cantine aperte is celebrated every May at over fifty wineries. Teramo dedicates a day (May 1) to its iconic dish, the Virtu. In July, the Festa del tartufo celebrates truffles, and in September, the Stefano di Sessanio celebrates its locally grown lentils.

Since the Middle Ages, the region has produced fine handicrafts which have graced the homes and tables of nobles and royals. The renowned Castelli pottery is showcased in many major art museums of the world including The Hermitage in Russia and the British

Museum. The tradition of pottery has not died and you can still pick a great pottery souvenir in Abruzzo.

Abruzzo is famous for its goldsmithing especially filigree (ornamental works in fine wire-like forms). Other forms of handicrafts to look for include woodwork, stone masonary, leatherwork, and textiles. The taranta, a heavy wool blanket typically made in the Abruzzo region, is famous all over Italy.

🌐 Geography

The Abruzzo region in central Italy is bordered by Marche on the north, Molise to the southeast, Lazio on the south and southwest, and the Adriatic Sea on the east. Geographically, the region is in central Italy but the Italian statistical authority lists it as part of southern Italy. The Italian capital of Rome is only about 120 km by road from

ABRUZZO TRAVEL GUIDE

the region's capital, L'Aquila. The region spans an expansive 10,763 sq km.

If you are planning to fly in to Abruzzo, then you will be using the only international airport in the region – the Abruzzo Airport, IATA: PSR - http://www.abruzzoairport.com/. The airport is located near the coast, about 4 km from the city of Pescara. It is served by Alitalia, Ryanair, and Wizzair, connecting the region directly with Barcelona, London, Frankfurt, Paris, Brussels and a number of Italian cities.

Taxis and airport shuttle buses are available near the airport terminal to go the town center. Direct bus lines are also available to Chieti, Naples, and Rome. There is also a train connection run by Trenitalia.

ABRUZZO TRAVEL GUIDE

Visitors may find it more convenient to fly into one of the international airports in Rome. Rome is served by the Fiumicino – Leonardo da Vinci International Airport, IATA: FCO - http://www.adr.it/fiumicino, and the Ciampino–G. B. Pastine International Airport, IATA: CIA - http://www.adr.it/ciampino.

The Fiumicino – Leonardo da Vinci International Airport is the main airport in Rome and has many connections to major cities across the globe. Ciampino Airport mostly handles many charter flights. From Rome, you can use the train, rental car, or bus to get to Abruzzo.

Train services, run by Trentitalia - http://www.trenitalia.com is not fastest means of travelling in Abruzzo, but some of the routes are so scenic that it makes up for the drawbacks. The train station in Pescara, the central station for the Abruzzo region, however, is considered one of the best in Europe. The train lines in service in the Abruzzo region include the Adriatic Railway line along the Adriatic coast; the Rome to Pescara line via Sulmona; the Sulmona to Carpinone line that passes through Brenner – the highest train station in the country; the Sulmona to Terni line; and the Giulianova to Teramo line.

The road network is extensively used in the Abruzzo region. Abruzzo is connected by the motorways – autostrade – A14, A24, A25. You can drive your own vehicle or use the long distance bus services - http://www.arpaonline.it/. The excellent condition of the roads is complemented by some stunning views of the Abruzzo landscape.

Within the Abruzzo region, the coast can be explored using the public bus or train service. The major cities and towns are connected by bus.

If you are planning to visit the interior, or remote villages, then it may be preferable to rent a car. Most of the towns in Abruzzo are quite small and can be covered by foot.

🌍 Weather & Best Time to Visit

The varied topography of the Apennine range and the Adriatic coast results in the Abruzzo region having diverse weather. The Adriatic coast has a Mediterranean climate with hot and dry summers and mild and wet winters. Temperatures reach an average high of 29 degrees Celsius in the summer months of May to October.

ABRUZZO TRAVEL GUIDE

The average low during this season is 16 to 18 degrees. In the winter months – between November and March – the average high is 10 degrees Celsius and the average low just above freezing. The mountain regions are slightly cooler with higher altitudes. Temperatures are lower by 3 to 4 degrees at both these extremes. The drier and sunnier summer days make this the best time to visit Abruzzo.

ABRUZZO TRAVEL GUIDE

Sights & Activities: What to See & Do

🌍 L'Aquila

With so many historic cities and towns representing the flavor and tradition of the region, visitors to Rome should take at least one day to enjoy the magic of L'Aquila.

L'Aquila is the capital of the Abruzzo region and is located near the northwestern borders of Abruzzo. It is about 110

ABRUZZO TRAVEL GUIDE

km by road from Rome and you can travel from Rome by bus, train, or by car in less than 2 hours.

A good place to start is the Fountain of the 99 Sprouts, one of the iconic landmarks of the city on Via Madonna del Ponte.

In close proximity are the medieval churches of San Silvestro and San Pietro di Coppito. Next stop is the mid 16th century Spanish fortress – Castello, which is also the home to the National Museum of Abruzzo. Very close to it is the St Bernardino Basilica, one of the most imposing Renaissance churches in the region.

After lunch take a walk in the city center (Portici) where you will see the town hall, medieval streets, and the

ABRUZZO TRAVEL GUIDE

historic architecture. Located near the square are the 13th century Piazza Duomo and Santa Maria di Collemaggio.

If you have time and a vehicle, head out to the Gran Sasso National Park where you can see the Rocca Calascio fortress, the highest in Italy.

🌍 Teramo

The city of Teramo is one of the most visited cities in Abruzzo. It is the capital of the Teramo Province. Teramo is located about 150 km east of the capital Rome, between the Apennine range and the coast of the Adriatic.

The city has breathtaking surrounding landscape, food, and historic architecture. The province of Teramo is known for its olive groves and vineyards.

ABRUZZO TRAVEL GUIDE

Teramo is well connected by road transport through the A14 and A24 motorways. If you are driving from Rome, you will be passing through the 10 km long tunnel through the Gran Sasso d'Italia – the highest mountain in Abruzzo – to reach the city. If you are coming by train, you will be using the station located about 1 km from downtown. Once in the city, you can see almost all the attractions by foot.

The city was inhabited from the pre-Roman times. It was earlier called Interamnia meaning "between the rivers" as the city is located at the confluence of the rivers Tordino and Vezzola. Although its fortunes grew during Roman times, it declined rapidly with the fall of the empire. The 14th and 15th centuries saw the city plagued by bloody feuds of rival families. A stone shield monument in the city center marks one such incident when 13 members of one

ABRUZZO TRAVEL GUIDE

family were brutally murdered. Teramo was united with Italy during the mid 19th century.

One of the best attractions in town is the Teramo Cathedral. This late 12th century Roman Catholic Cathedral was built in a Romanesque Gothic style and is dedicated to the Assumption of the Virgin Mary and St Berado, the patron saint of Teramo. It was commissioned to house the relics of the patron saint. The church has seen a number of alterations over the years but its original medieval look was restored in the 1930s.

The church is easily identified by its wide façade and the tall bell tower to its right. The church is of artistic as well as religious significance. Look for the silver antependium near the altar and an impressive polyptych with images from the life of Jesus.

ABRUZZO TRAVEL GUIDE

Other notable churches in the city include the early 12th century St Antonio Church, the 14th century San Domenico Church, and the ruins of the mid 12th century San Getulio Church. The sanctuary of Madonna delle Graze is also revered by pilgrims for its miraculous 15th century wood statue of Virgin Mary.

The city prospered under the Romans and you can still see some ruins from that era. The city center has the ruins of the 2nd century Roman theater. The theater, which is today almost 3 metres below the encircling road, once could accommodate 3000 spectators.

In close proximity you can see the ruins of an amphitheater. Nearby is the Torre Bruciata, the Burnt

ABRUZZO TRAVEL GUIDE

Tower, which was built by the Romans around the 2nd century BC.

Other places of interest in Teramo include the Bishop's Palace near Liberty Square, and the 12th century Melatino House. Visit the F. Savini Archeological Museum housed in the former Church of San Carlo.

Check out the beaches of Teramo. The golden sands, beach resorts, water activities, and lively nightlife make Teramo one of the most fun places in Abruzzo.

If you have time, take a relaxing drive to see the "Seven Sisters" which are seven towns along Teramo's 60 km long coastline. The towns include Silvi, Pineto, Roseto degli Abruzzi, Giulianova, Tortoreto, Alba Adriatica, and Martinsicuro.

The city hosts the Maggio Festeggiante art festival every May. In October, Teramo hosts an international film festival. Sports lovers can attend the Interamnia World Cup of handball during the summertime.

The city produces some of the finest wine and olive oil in Abruzzo as well as Millefiori mountain honey. The locally made pecorino marcetto cheese is known for its strong flavor and smell. Meat lovers should try the ventricia teramana, a type of salami. A variety of seafood can also be tried along the coast. If you are visiting during Christmas, do not miss the traditional stockfish.

🌎 Sulmona

Located in the province of L'Aquila, Sulmona is one of the most picturesque towns in Abruzzo. It is situated at the

ABRUZZO TRAVEL GUIDE

confluence of the Rivers Vella and Gizio. Imposing mountains create the backdrop for this historic city. The city has been devastated by many earthquakes and wars but has preserved many of its historic buildings and monuments.

Today, one of Sulmona's claims to fame is its confetti, a type of Italian confectionery made with sugarcoated almonds. It is also renowned for its goldsmith's art, which can be seen in many museums and galleries in Italy. Sulmona is the hometown of the legendary poet Ovid.

Sulmona is well connected by rail and road transport from Rome, Pescara, and Tivoli. The 3 hour train ride from Rome is one of the most spectacular in the region and has breathtaking scenery. Quicker options are to take the bus (about 2 hours) or rental car (about 1.5 hours). If you are driving, avoid parking in the city center; there is a free car park just outside the center near the fire station. The city has a public bus service and a number of taxis and can be easily covered by foot.

Attractions in Sulmona include the Sulmona Cathedral. This Romanesque styled church has a Byzantine relief depicting the Virgin with her Child, and a beautiful 15th century sarcophagi. The Annunziata Palace is one of those fine examples of Renaissance architecture that survived the devastating earthquake of 1706. Its beauty lies in its finely sculpted façade. The Palace houses the Civico Archeologico Museum displaying images and artifacts on the Roman history of the city. The Baroque-styled Annunziata Church is popular for its impressive bell tower and beautifully crafted interior.

ABRUZZO TRAVEL GUIDE

The Piazza Garibaldi, with its Baroque fountain, is the largest square in the city. It is one of the most popular sites for festivals and gatherings. The square is especially crowded during the annual horse race, the medieval festival, and during the Easter parade. There is a 12th century Gothic styled aqueduct on its southern flank. You can visit the markets in the square on Wednesdays and Saturdays. The Piazza XX Setembre is another popular square in the city. It has a bronze statue of Sulmona's most famous son, Ovid.

Just outside the gates of Sulmona you will see the ruins of an ancient theater, amphitheater, and Roman bath. About 3 km from the city center, at Monte Morrone, you will see the ruins of the Hercules Curinus sanctuary. Close to the sanctuary, you can see the ruins of a former hermitage and convent.

ABRUZZO TRAVEL GUIDE

When in Sulmona, you should try the famous confetti. Often, these candies (sweets) are used as decorations. There are many shops all over the city selling confetti. There is also a mini museum dedicated to this delicacy.

🌍 Pescara

Pescara has a population of 125,000 making it the largest city in Abruzzo. The city is a beautiful seaside resort with a sweeping beach promenade and a long stretch of pedestrianised street.

You can fly directly to Pescara's Abruzzo Airport which is located 5 km from the city center. Pescara also has regular rail connections. The city has 4 train stations and Pescale Centrale is the main station. You can take direct train connections from many Italian cities including

ABRUZZO TRAVEL GUIDE

L'Aquila, Milan, Venice, Bari, Turin, and Rome. Pescara also has ferry connections from Split and Dalmatia in Croatia during the summer months.

Once in this charming town, you can see most of it by foot, especially as most of the action is at or near the beaches.

One of the most visited attractions in Pescara is the house of Gabriel D'Annunzio, the renowned Italian poet and journalist.

Other places of interest include the San Cetteo Cathedral with its marble mausoleum of D'Annunnzio's mother, and a 17th century painting of Guercino. The city also has the historic Spirito Santo Church and the Sant'Andrea Apostolo Church. The impressive Governor's Palace is home to many beautifully crafted statues along with the impressive 'La Figlia di Iorio' painting by Michetti. Pescara has a number of museums including the Museo delle Genti d'Abruzzo, the Museo Cascella, and the Museo Ittico.

The city's most popular event is the month long Madonna dei Setti Dolori Festival in summer. In July, the St Andrea the Apostle's feast is accompanied by a parade of fishing boats.

Art and music lovers will enjoy the International Jazz festival and the Ennio Flaiano prize in audio-visual entertainment, both held in July.

The city is also a living gallery with many art installations all over the city, including the seaside promenade at

ABRUZZO TRAVEL GUIDE

Piazza Salotto. The picturesque La Bella Dormenteta Mountain is just 40 minutes drive away.

Pescara is famous for its beaches, which are the epicenter for partiers and nightlife-lovers. There are a number of discos and clubs along the coast. In the winter months, the parties move to the university area and Corso Montheone. In Pescara you can dance the night away or just people-watch from one of the laid-back beach cafes.

🌏 Chieti

The city of Chieti is a beautiful city cradled between the Adriatic coast and the Gran Sasso and Majella Mountains. It is situated on the banks of the River Pescara. The city is believed to be one of the oldest in Italy. According to myth, Chieti was founded in 1181BC by Achilles. Chieti was originally called Teate and grew rapidly under Roman

ABRUZZO TRAVEL GUIDE

rule. There are many monuments and ruins preserved from that era.

The city is located under 200 km from Rome. It can be reached by taking a scenic drive on the SS5 road and the A25 motorway.

Chieti has a number of medieval churches and cathedrals. One of the most popular is the Chieti Cathedral. Originally built in the 11th century, the cathedral was rebuilt in the 18th century in a Gothic style. The Romanesque-styled crypt from the original church and the impressive bell tower from the 14th century still remain.

The 12th century St Francesco Church has a Baroque façade, beautiful rose-covered windows, and paintings by Spinelli and Graziani.

ABRUZZO TRAVEL GUIDE

The St Giustino Cathedral is a work of art of itself with an impressive bell tower, stunning marble altar, prized wooden furniture, and many frescoes and paintings.

Other churches with impressive works of art include the Church of St Giovanni Battista and Chiesa di S. Gaetano. History buffs should visit the S. Pietro e Paolo Church where excavations have revealed brickwork and a reservoir from the Roman era.

The city has many museums including the National Archelogical Museum, Diocesan Theatine Museum, La Civitella Art Museum, Palazzo de Mayo Art Museum, Biomedical Science Museum, and the Barbella Art Museum.

🌐 National Parks

Abruzzo is blessed with lush greenery making it the greenest region of Europe. One third of Abruzzo is covered by National Parks. The three National Parks and many of the natural reserves in Abruzzo have a variety of flora due to the elevation ranging from 600 m to over 2000 m. The fauna is also as varied including the viper, porcupine, otter, badger, wildcat, lynx, marsican brown bear, and Italian wolf.

The National Park of Abruzzo was founded in 1922 and covers 497 sq km. The largest park is the mostly mountainous Gran Sasso and Monte Della National Park, spanning 2014 sq km. It is one of the most diverse biological areas in Europe. The park has over 300 km of trails for hiking, horseriding and mountain biking.

The Maiella National Park – spanning 741 sq km – is very scenic and has numerous hiking trails. It is home to a number of important archeological sites including caves with cave paintings.

Castles & Fortresses

The Abruzzo region is dotted with many medieval castles and fortresses. Many of these can be seen when driving through the mountain roads. From the SS5 near L'Aquila, you will see the San Pio Delle Camere. Built on a hillside it once protected the town just a few hundred feet below. Farther down the SS5 is the Ocre castle (with acropolis and church) nestled on the hilltop.

The Renaissance-styled Celano Castle was once the manor house of a noble. Eastwards, on SS5, you will see

ABRUZZO TRAVEL GUIDE

the Castelvecchio Subequo – a fortified village that has been preserved over the centuries.

Nearby, on the SS261, is the castle town of Fontecchio. The clock tower of the castle is one of the oldest clocks in the country. The 14th century Rocca Calsacio has stunning panoramic views of the surrounding mountains and valleys. Similar breathtaking views can be seen from the Santo Stefano Castle.

ABRUZZO TRAVEL GUIDE

🌎 Recommended Itinerary: Two Days in Abruzzo

If you have only two days to get a feel for Abruzzo start by renting a car and take a unforgettable road trip.

See L'Aquila and then head to the Gran Sasso National Park. Taking the A24, you will pass Castelli, one of the best places to buy handcrafted ceramics in Abruzzo.

ABRUZZO TRAVEL GUIDE

Take the SS150 to reach Atri which has a magnificent 9th century cathedral and a Roman Bath with some of the finest frescoes in Abruzzo. From the SS150, take the coastal route of SS16 to reach Pescara.

Enjoy Pescara with its medieval churches standing side by side with modern structures like the Fater SPA Headquarters. Spend the night at Pescara.

Next morning, take SS5 towards Chieti, less than 20 km away. One of the most ancient cities of Italy, Chieti has a number of medieval churches and some very good museums. From Chieti, a drive back to L'Aquila will take about 2 hours on the SS5 and SS17.

ABRUZZO TRAVEL GUIDE

Budget Tips

🌐 Accommodation

Hotel Rojan

Via Deghli Aghiacciati 15

67039 Sulmona

Tel: 39 0864 950 126

http://www.hotelrojan.it/en_index.htm

This is a 4 star hotel located in a historic district of Sulmona. All the major attractions are within walking distance from the hotel.

The hotel has free parking, can arrange for shuttle service, and has facilities for disabled guests. It has a travel desk and bicycle rental facilities for its guests. There is an onsite bar and lounge.

The ensuite rooms have Wi-Fi, cable TV, electronic safe, remote controlled thermostat, hair dryer, complimentary toiletries, and a balcony with great views of the surrounding historic quarter. Room rates start from €90 and include breakfast.

Albergo Stella

Via Mazara 18

Sulmona

Tel: 39 0864 52653

http://www.albergostella.info/?lang=en

This is a clean and cozy hotel located in the old town center of Sulmona. It offers free parking in the old center for its guests. This pet friendly hotel has free Wi-Fi throughout. It can arrange for shuttle services to all major attractions in town. The hotel also has an onsite bar and restaurant.

The ensuite rooms have AC, cable TV, newspaper, safe, toiletries and hairdryer. Room rates start from €40 and include breakfast.

Hotel Alba

Via Michaelangelo Forti 14

65122 Pescara

Tel: 39 085 389 145

http://www.hotelalbapescara.com/

This is a 3 star hotel housed in a refurbished early 20th century building. It is located close to the city attractions with the beach just 200 m away. This non-smoking hotel has 24 hour reception, family room, facilities for disabled guests, and concierge service. It allows pets. There is an onsite bar and restaurant.

The beautifully decorated ensuite rooms have AC, cable TV, free Wi-Fi, hairdryer, minibar, safe. Room rates start from €45.

Hotel Gran Sasso

Via Vinciguerra 12

64100 Teramo

Tel: 39 0861 245 747

http://www.hotelgransassoteramo.eu/

This is a 3 star hotel located in Teramo's historic center. It is located 10 km from the Gran Sasso and Monte della Laga National Park. The hotel has 24 hour front desk, free parking, family rooms, and concierge service. Pets are allowed. There is an onsite bar and restaurant. It also has a vending machine for snacks.

The ensuite rooms have AC, cable TV, free Wi-Fi, and all other basic amenities. Room rates start from €36.

Harri's Hotel Chieti

Via P A Valignani 219

66100 Chieti

Tel: 39 0871 321 555

http://www.harrishotels.it/

This is a 4 star hotel located just a km away from the popular historic center of Chieti. There is a bus stop across the road from the hotel. The hotel, being located on a hillside, has panoramic views of the surroundings. It has family rooms and facilities for disabled guests. It can arrange for shuttle services to and from the airport. There is an onsite restaurant and bar, and wellness center. Pets are allowed.

The ensuite rooms have AC, cable TV, free Wi-Fi, minibar, safe, and a large balcony. Room rates start from €60.

Places to Eat

Carbonera

Viale della Riviera 20

65123 Pescara

Tel: 39 085 943 2518

http://www.carbonerarestaurant.it/

This is an elegant restaurant located close to the Piazza I Maggio. It has large windows through which you can see the Adriatic Sea. In the summer months, you can dine al fresco. This restaurant cum bar specializes in local cuisine.

The restaurant specialises in local seafood. Some of the house specialties include sea bass carpaccio, tuna carpaccio, salmon almond pie, and cuttlefish with roasted peppers. The restaurant can accommodate large groups.

La Terrazze

Piazza Primo Maggio 46

65122 Pescara

Tel: 39 085 943 1337

http://www.leterrazzepescara.com/en/

La Terrazze is located on the top floor of an Art Deco styled building on the seafront. The elegantly decorated interior is complemented by excellent service, breathtaking views, and delicious food. You can dine indoors and enjoy the views through the French windows or dine al fresco on the terrace. The Mediterranean cuisine that is served is prepared with extreme detail. It also has a lounge bar in the main dining room.

La Cucina di Lullo

Via Colonnetta 99

66100 Chieti

Tel: 39 333 325 6513

http://www.lacucinadilullo.it/

Located on the ground floor of a building, this is one of the best places in Chieti to try authentic local cuisine.

Dishes are prepared with fresh local ingredients. The tidy interior and low prices make the place highly recommended.

Some of the house specialties of the restaurant are also the unique dishes of the region like the sheep callara, pallotte cheese and eggs, lu ciabbott. Try the 'Pizza and Fuje' – a maize pizza filled with vegetables. The restaurant also has a good collection of wines.

Riva Reno

Via Venezia 14

Pescara

Tel: 39 085 27 001

http://www.rivareno.com/eng/

This is a place for those who love desserts, especially ice

cream. It serves many varieties of gelatos, sorbets, and granitas. There are 15 flavors of gelatos made from the highest quality milk, cream, carob flour, and cane sugar. The fruit sorbet is dairy-free and made with fresh seasonal fruits, carob flour, and cane sugar. The Granita – a Sicilian delicacy – is made with seasonal fruits, water, and sugar, and is devoid of any artificial color or aroma. Special care is taken in storing the ice cream in traditional cylindrical containers so as to retain its taste.

Ristorante Pizzeria bar II Sarto Imbocca

Via per Popoli 265

66100 Chieti

Tel: 39 327 222 8952

https://www.facebook.com/ilsarto.imbocca.7

ABRUZZO TRAVEL GUIDE

Ristorante Pizzeria bar Il Sarto Imbocca serves Italian dishes like pizza, calzone, and pasta. This is where you can taste these foods at their authentic best. The excellent service, sizeable portions, and nice ambience add to the dining experience. The restaurant also serves focaccia, salads, and antipasti. The Pallotte cheese with eggs, mushroom dishes, and cakes are recommended.

Shopping

Confetti of Sulmona

Via S Introdacqua 23

67039 Sulmona

Tel: 39 0864 55 077

http://www.confettisulmona.net/bomboniere/index.php?route=common/home

Sulmona is famous all over Italy for its confetti and this is one of the best places in town to buy this almond delicacy. This store sells a wide variety of confetti in all shapes and sizes.

You can find confetti sweets shaped like marbles or a flower. There are flavors and designs for occasions like baptisms, weddings, and graduations. Visit the store to buy some confetti as a souvenir or for gifts.

Chieti

Chieti is known for its fine wine shops. One of the popular wineries is Frattoria Licia. You can also buy excellent local olive oil at Agricola Tommaso Masciantonio. There is a traditional fresh food market at the Municipal Square every Tuesday.

ABRUZZO TRAVEL GUIDE

L'Aquila

L'Aquila has a number of outdoor markets and traditional food markets where you can buy locally made cheese, freshly-baked bread, olive oil, and wine. The city has many good bakeries and patisseries. The red wine and traditional pastries are especially recommended.

Antique Shopping

Many cities in Abruzzo have a flea and antiques market. In L'Aquila, the flea market is open on the 2nd weekend of every month. In Sulmona and Pescara, the annual flea market is held in July.

In Papoli there is an annual street flea market held every August. In Castelli, there is a flea market every July and August along with a display of locally-made ceramic products.

Centro D'Abruzzo

Centro D'Abruzzo is a major shopping mall located between Chieti and Pescara and a large retail park has developed onsite. The mall is a great place to buy local and branded products as well as souvenirs of the Abruzzo region.

ABRUZZO TRAVEL GUIDE

Know Before You Go

🌐 Entry Requirements

By virtue of the Schengen agreement, travellers from other countries in the European Union do not need a visa when visiting Italy. Additionally Swiss travellers are also exempt. Visitors from certain other countries such as the USA, Canada, Japan, Israel, Australia and New Zealand do not need visas if their stay in Italy does not exceed 90 days. When entering Italy you will be required to make a declaration of presence, either at the airport, or at a police station within eight days of arrival. This applies to visitors from other Schengen countries, as well as those visiting from non-Schengen countries.

🌐 Health Insurance

Citizens of other EU countries are covered for emergency health care in Italy. UK residents, as well as visitors from Switzerland are covered by the European Health Insurance Card (EHIC), which can be applied for free of charge. Visitors from non-Schengen countries will need to show proof of private health insurance that is valid for the duration of their stay in Italy (that offers at least €37,500 coverage), as part of their visa application. No special vaccinations are required.

🌐 Travelling with Pets

Italy participates in the Pet Travel Scheme (PETS) which allows UK residents to travel with their pets without requiring quarantine upon re-entry. Certain conditions will need to be met. The animal will have to be microchipped and up to date on rabies vaccinations. In the case of dogs, a vaccination against canine distemper is also required by the Italian authorities. When travelling from the USA, your pet will need to be microchipped or marked with an identifying tattoo and up to date on rabies vaccinations. An EU Annex IV Veterinary Certificate for Italy will need to be issued by an accredited veterinarian. On arrival in Italy, you can apply for an EU pet passport to ease your travel in other EU countries.

🌐 Airports

Fiumicino – Leonardo da Vinci International Airport (FCO) is one of the busiest airports in Europe and the main international airport of Italy. It is located about 35km southwest of the historical quarter of Rome. Terminal 5 is used for trans-

ABRUZZO TRAVEL GUIDE

Atlantic and international flights, while Terminals 1, 2 and 3 serve mainly for domestic flights and medium haul flights to other European destinations. Before Leonardo da Vinci replaced it, the **Ciampino–G. B. Pastine International Airport** (CIA) was the main international airport servicing Rome and Italy. It is one of the oldest airports in the country still in use. Although it declined in importance, budget airlines such as Ryanair boosted its air traffic in recent years. The airport is used by Wizz Air, V Bird, Helvetic, Transavia Airlines, Sterling, Ryanair, Thomsonfly, EasyJet, Air Berlin, Hapag-Lloyd Express and Carpatair.

Milan Malpensa Airport (MXP) is the largest of the three airports serving the city of Milan. Located about 40km northwest of Milan's city center, it connects travellers to the regions of Lombardy, Piedmont and Liguria. **Milan Linate Airport** (LIN) is Milan's second international airport. **Venice Marco Polo Airport** (VCE) provides access to the charms of Venice. **Olbia Costa Smeralda Airport** (OLB) is located near Olbia, Sardinia. Main regional airports are **Guglielmo Marconi Airport** (BLQ), an international airport servicing the region of Bologna, **Capodichino Airport** at Naples (NAP), **Pisa International Airport** (PSA), formerly Galileo Galilei Airport, the main airport serving Tuscany, **Sandro Pertini Airport** near Turin (TRN), **Cristoforo Colombo** in Genoa (GOA), **Punta Raisi Airport** in Palermo (PMO), **Vincenzo Bellini Airport** in Catania (CTA) and **Palese Airport** in Bari (BRI).

🌎 Airlines

Alitalia is the flag carrier and national airline of Italy. It has a subsidiary, Alitalia CityLiner, which operates short-haul regional flights. Air Dolomiti is a regional Italian based subsidiary of of the Lufthansa Group. Meridiana is a privately owned airline based at Olbia in Sardinia.

Fiumicino - Leonardo da Vinci International Airport serves as the main hub for Alitalia, which has secondary hubs at Milan Linate and Milan Malpensa Airport. Alitalia CityLiner uses Fiumicino – Leonardo da Vinci International Airport as main hub and has secondary hubs at Milan-Linate, Naples and Trieste. Fiumicino – Leonardo da Vinci International Airport is also one of two primary hubs used by the budget Spanish airline Vueling. Milan Malpensa Airport is one of the largest bases for the British budget airline EasyJet. Venice Airport serves as an Italian base for the Spanish budget airline, Volotea, which provides connections mainly to other destinations in Europe. Olbia Costa Smeralda Airport (OLB), located near Olbia, Sardinia is the primary base of Meridiana, a private Italian Airline in partnership with Air Italia and Fly Egypt.

🌎 Currency

Italy's currency is the Euro. It is issued in notes in denominations of €500, €200, €100, €50, €20, €10 and €5.

Coins are issued in denominations of €2, €1, 50c, 20c, 10c, 5c, 2c and 1c.

🌎 Banking & ATMs

Using ATMs or Bancomats, as they are known in Italy, to withdraw money is simple if your ATM card is compatible with the MasterCard/Cirrus or Visa/Plus networks. There is a €250 limit on daily withdrawals. Italian machines are configured for 4-digit PIN numbers, although some machines will be able to handle longer PIN numbers. Bear in mind some Bancomats can run out of cash over weekends and that the more remote villages may not have adequate banking facilities so plan ahead.

🌎 Credit Cards

Credit cards are valid tender in most Italian businesses. While Visa and MasterCard are accepted universally, most tourist oriented businesses also accept American Express and Diners Club. Credit cards issued in Europe are smart cards that that are fitted with a microchip and require a PIN for each transaction. This means that a few ticket machines, self-service vendors and other businesses may not be configured to accept the older magnetic strip credit cards. Do remember to advise your bank or credit card company of your travel plans before leaving.

🌐 Tourist Taxes

Tourist tax varies from city to city, as each municipality sets its own rate. The money is collected by your accommodation and depends on the standard of accommodation. A five star establishment will levy a higher amount than a four star or three star establishment. You can expect to pay somewhere between €1 and €7 per night, with popular destinations like Rome, Venice, Milan and Florence charging a higher overall rate. In some regions, the rate is also adjusted seasonally. Children are usually exempt until at least the age of 10 and sometimes up to the age of 18. In certain areas, disabled persons and their companions also qualify for discounted rates. Tourist tax is payable directly to the hotel or guesthouse before the end of your stay.

🌐 Reclaiming VAT

If you are not from the European Union, you can claim back VAT (Value Added Tax) paid on your purchases in Italy. The VAT rate in Italy is 21 percent and this can be claimed back on your purchases if certain conditions are met. The merchant needs to be partnered with a VAT refund program. This will be indicated if the shop displays a "Tax Free" sign. The shop assistant will fill out a form for reclaiming VAT. When you submit this at the airport, you will receive your refund.

🌐 Tipping Policy

If your bill includes the phrase "coperto e servizio", that means that a service charge or tip is already included. Most waiting staff in Italy are salaried workers, but if the service is excellent, a few euros extra would be appreciated.

🌐 Mobile Phones

Most EU countries, including Italy use the GSM mobile service. This means that most UK phones and some US and Canadian phones and mobile devices will work in Italy. While you could check with your service provider about coverage before you leave, using your own service in roaming mode will involve additional costs. The alternative is to purchase an Italian SIM card to use during your stay in Italy.

Italy has four mobile networks. They are TIM, Wind, Vodafone and Tre (3) and they all provide pre-paid services. TIM offers two tourist options, both priced at €20 (+ €10 for the SIM card) with a choice of two packages - 2Gb data, plus 200 minutes call time or internet access only with a data allowance of 5Gb. Vodafone, Italy's second largest network offers a Vodafone Holiday package including SIM card for €30. They also offer the cheapest roaming rates. Wind offers an Italian Tourist pass for €20 which includes 100 minutes call time and 2Gb data and can be extended with a restart option for an extra €10.

To purchase a local SIM card, you will need to show your passport or some other form of identification and provide your residential details in Italy. By law, SIM registration is required prior to activation. Most Italian SIM cards expire after a 90 day period of inactivity. When dialling internationally, remember to use the (+) sign and the code of the country you are connecting to.

🌐 Dialling Code

The international dialling code for Italy is +39.

🌐 Emergency Numbers

Police: 113
Fire: 115
Ambulance: 118
MasterCard: 800 789 525
Visa: 800 819 014

🌐 Public Holidays

1 January: New Year's Day (Capodanno)
6 January: Day of the Epiphany (Epifania)
March-April: Easter Monday (Lunedì dell'Angelo or Pasquetta)
25 April: Liberation Day (Festa della Liberazione)

ABRUZZO TRAVEL GUIDE

1 May: International Worker's Day (Festa del Lavoro / Festa dei Lavoratori)

2 June: Republic Day (Festa della Repubblica)

15 August: Assumption Day (Ferragosto / Assunta)

1 November: All Saints Day (Tutti i santi / Ognissanti)

8 December: Immaculate Conception (Immacolata Concezione / Immacolata)

25 December: Christmas Day (Natale)

26 December: St Stephen's Day (Santo Stefano)

A number of Saints days are observed regionally throughout the year.

🌐 Time Zone

Italy falls in the Central European Time Zone. This can be calculated as Greenwich Mean Time/Coordinated Universal Time (GMT/UTC) +2; Eastern Standard Time (North America) -6; Pacific Standard Time (North America) -9.

🌐 Daylight Savings Time

Clocks are set forward one hour on 29 March and set back one hour on 25 October for Daylight Savings Time.

ABRUZZO TRAVEL GUIDE

🌏 School Holidays

The academic year begins in mid September and ends in mid June. The summer holiday is from mid June to mid September, although the exact times may vary according to region. There are short breaks around Christmas and New Year and also during Easter. Some regions such as Venice and Trentino have an additional break during February for the carnival season.

🌏 Trading Hours

Trading hours for the majority of shops are from 9am to 12.30pm and then again from 3.30pm to 7.30pm, although in some areas, the second shift may be from 4pm to 8pm instead. The period between 1pm and 4pm is known in Italy as the *riposo*. Large department shops and malls tend to be open from 9am to 9pm, from Monday to Saturday. Post offices are open from 8.30am to 1.30pm from Monday to Saturday. Most shops and many restaurants are closed on Sundays. Banking hours are from 8.30am to 1.30pm and then again from 3pm to 4pm, Monday to Friday. Most restaurants are open from noon till 2.30pm and then again from 7pm till 11pm or midnight, depending on the establishment. Nightclubs open around 10pm, but only liven up after midnight. Closing times vary, but will generally be between 2am and 4am. Museum hours vary, although major sights tend to be open continuously and often up to 7.30pm. Many museums are closed on Mondays.

🌐 Driving Laws

The Italians drive on the right hand side of the road. A driver's licence from any of the European Union member countries is valid in Italy. Visitors from non-EU countries will require an International Driving Permit that must remain current throughout the duration of their stay in Italy.

The speed limit on Italy's autostrade is 130km per hour and 110km per hour on main extra-urban roads, but this is reduced by 20km to 110km and 90km respectively in rainy weather. On secondary extra-urban roads, the speed limit is 90km per hour; on urban highways, it is 70km per hour and on urban roads, the speed limit is 50km per hour. You are not allowed to drive in the ZTL or Limited Traffic Zone (or *zona traffico limitato* in Italian) unless you have a special permit.

Visitors to Italy are allowed to drive their own non-Italian vehicles in the country for a period of up to six months. After this, they will be required to obtain Italian registration with Italian licence plates. Italy has very strict laws against driving under the influence of alcohol. The blood alcohol limit is 0.05 and drivers caught above the limit face penalties such as fines of up to €6000, confiscation of their vehicles, suspension of their licenses and imprisonment of up to 6 months. Breathalyzer tests are routine at accident scenes.

🌎 Drinking Laws

The legal drinking age in Italy is 16. While drinking in public spaces is allowed, public drunkenness is not tolerated. Alcohol is sold in bars, wine shops, liquor stores and grocery shops.

🌎 Smoking Laws

In 2005, Italy implemented a policy banning smoking from public places such as bars, restaurants, nightclubs and working places, limiting it to specially designated smoking rooms. Further legislation banning smoking from parks, beaches and stadiums is being explored.

🌎 Electricity

Electricity: 220 volts

Frequency: 50 Hz

Italian electricity sockets are compatible with the Type L plugs, a plug that features three round pins or prongs, arranged in a straight line. An alternate is the two-pronged Type C Euro adaptor. If travelling from the USA, you will need a power converter or transformer to convert the voltage from 220 to 110, to avoid damage to your appliances. The latest models of many laptops, camcorders, mobile phones and digital cameras are dual-voltage with a built in converter.

🌎 Tourist Information (TI)

There are tourist information (TI) desks at each of the terminals of the Leonardo da Vinci International Airport, as well as interactive Information kiosks with the latest touch-screen technology. In Rome, the tourist office can be found at 5 Via Parigi, near the Termini Station and it is identified as APT, which stands for Azienda provinciale del Turismo. Free maps and brochures of current events are available from tourist kiosks.

Several of the more tourist-oriented regions of Italy offer tourist cards that include admission to most of the city's attractions. While these cards are not free, some offer great value for money. A variety of tourism apps are also available online.

🌎 Food & Drink

Pasta is a central element of many typically Italian dishes, but there are regional varieties and different types of pasta are matched to different sauces. Well known pasta dishes such as lasagne and bolognaise originated in Bologna. Stuffed pasta is popular in the northern part of Italy, while the abundance of

ABRUZZO TRAVEL GUIDE

seafood and olives influences southern Italian cuisine. As far as pizza goes, the Italians differentiate between the thicker Neapolitan pizza and the thin crust Roman pizza, as well as white pizza, also known as focaccia and tomato based pizza. Other standards include minestrone soup, risotto, polenta and a variety of cheeses, hams, sausages and salamis. If you are on a budget, consider snacking on stuzzichini with a few drinks during happy hour which is often between 7 and 9pm. The fare can include salami, cheeses, cured meat, mini pizzas, bread, vegetables, pastries or pate. In Italy, Parmesan refers only to cheese originating from the area surrounding Parma. Favorites desserts include tiramisu or Italian gelato.

Italians enjoy relaxing to aperitifs before they settle down to a meal and their favorites are Campari, Aperol or Negroni, the famous Italian cocktail. Wine is enjoyed with dinner. Italy is particularly famous for its red wines. The best known wine regions are Piedmont, which produces robust and dry reds, Tuscany and Alto Adige, where Alpine soil adds a distinctive acidity. After the meal, they settle down to a glass of limoncello, the country's most popular liqueur, or grappa, which is distilled from grape seeds and stems, as digestive. Other options in this class include a nut liqueur, nocino, strawberry based Fragolino Veneto or herbal digestives like gineprino, laurino or mirto. Italians are also fond of coffee. Espresso is drunk through throughout the day, but cappuccino is considered a morning drink. The most popular beers in Italy are Peroni and Moretti.

🌐 Websites

http://vistoperitalia.esteri.it/home/en

This is the website of the Consulate General of Italy. Here you can look up whether you will need a visa and also process your application online.

http://www.italia.it/en/home.html

The official website of Italian tourism

http://www.italia.it/en/useful-info/mobile-apps.html

Select the region of your choice to download a useful mobile app to your phone.

http://www.italylogue.com/tourism

http://italiantourism.com/index.html

http://www.reidsitaly.com/

http://wikitravel.org/en/Italy

https://www.summerinitaly.com/

http://www.accessibleitalianholiday.com/

Planning Italian vacations around the needs of disabled tourists.

Printed in Great Britain
by Amazon